RUBANK EDUCATIONAL LIBRARY No. 53

RUBANK Elementary METHOD

VIOLA

SYLVAN D. WARD

A FUNDAMENTAL COURSE FOR INDIVIDUAL OR LIKE-INSTRUMENT CLASS INSTRUCTION

RUBANK®

HAL•LEONARD®

HOW TO HOLD THE VIOLA AND BOW

The illustration to the left shows the correct manner of holding the viola and bow with the bow on the string in playing position. Observe the natural position of the right hand and arm, the tapering fingers and relaxed wrist. The hair of the bow, you will see, faces the bridge on the instrument. Notice the left arm is held well under the Viola. See how nicely the fingers lay on the strings, and that the wrist is in a normal position. Stand or sit straight and do not allow yourself to stoop.

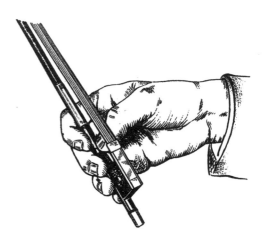

The above illustration shows the correct position of the left hand. See the curved position of the fingers on the string. The neck of the instrument is suspended between the thumb and the first finger and does not lay in the fleshy part of the hand. Notice the natural position of the wrist. Study this illustration closely.

The above illustration shows the correct manner of holding the bow. Observe the curved position of the thumb and that the bow fits in the second joint of the forefinger. The other fingers taper along the top of the stick with the little finger barely touching.

HOW TO TUNE

The names of the strings are "A" (which is the highest), "D", "G", and "C". Notice Viola music is written in Viola (or Alto) clef. The staff on the right shows the corresponding notes on the piano. Tune the strings to these notes.

39118-47

LEARNING TO BOW ON THE OPEN STRINGS

The exercises on this page are to enable you to get the "feel" of the bow, and to draw it straight (parallel with the bridge.) Note values and counting will be taken up on the next page.

In regard to playing the first note: Sometimes a better position of the arm can be acquired by starting the first note with an upbow instead of a downbow. This way you are able to determine immediately how long a bow you can draw and still keep it parallel with the bridge. Try it.

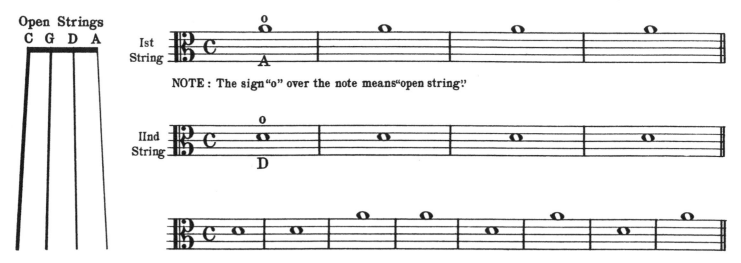

NOTE : The sign "o" over the note means "open string."

Check up on the way you are holding the bow. Are you curving your thumb correctly?

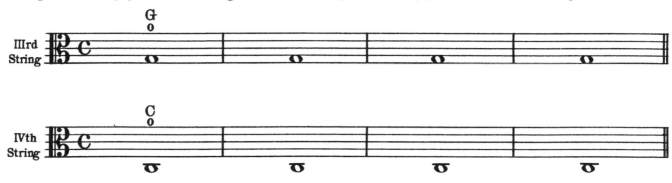

Are you drawing the bow straight?

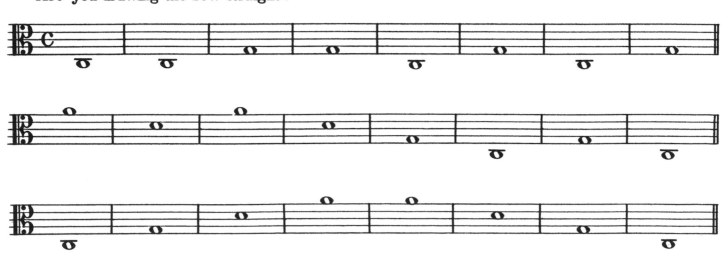

HALF NOTES AND HALF RESTS

If it is your preference to take up quarter notes before half notes, start at lower half of page.

QUARTER NOTES AND QUARTER RESTS
(Count one beat to each)

Use most of the bow but draw it straight.

OPEN STRING DANCE

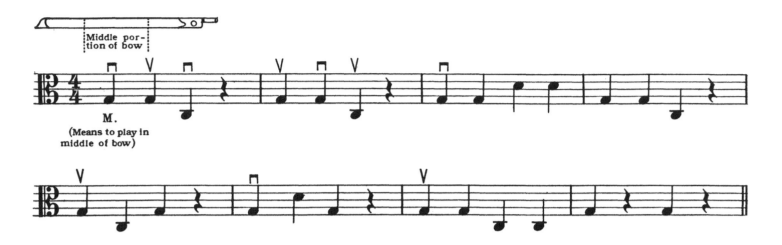

WHOLE NOTES AND WHOLE RESTS

Work for a nice full tone — Don't press hard on the bow

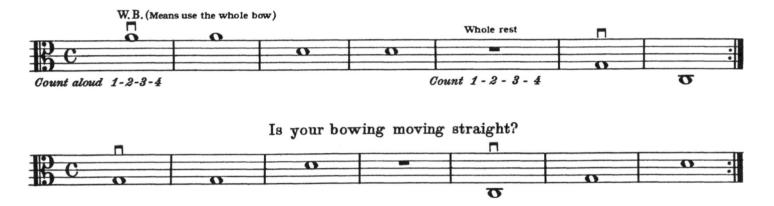

TONE STUDY OF HALF NOTES AND WHOLE NOTES

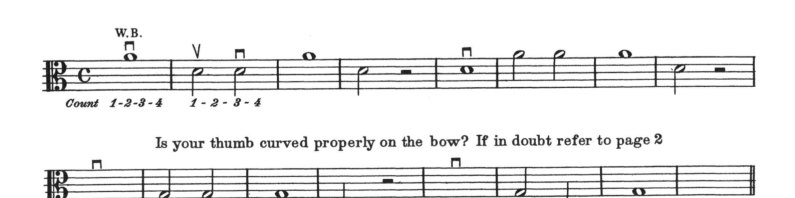

REVIEW OF HALF NOTES, QUARTER NOTES, WHOLE NOTES AND RESTS

4/4 Time - 4 beats to a measure, each quarter note gets one beat.

Count 1 - 2 - 3 - 4   1 - 2 - 3 - 4

L.H. means use lower half of bow. U.H. means upper half.

Same as 4/4 time

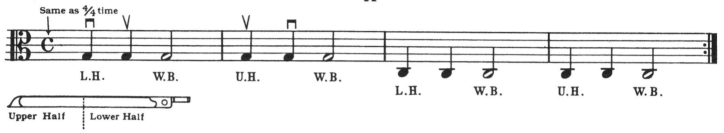

Upper Half | Lower Half

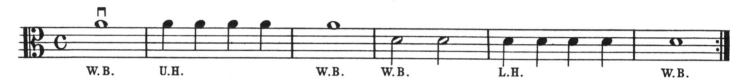

USING THE FIRST FINGER

Place your finger down solidly but don't allow the joint to cave.

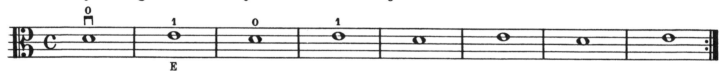

Is your bow moving straight?

Is your left hand in the correct position?

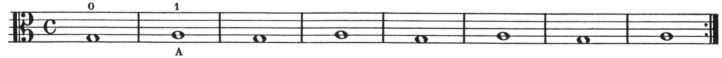

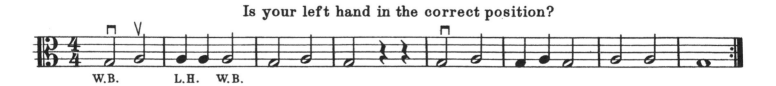

39118

FIRST FINGER EXERCISE

Learn the names of the your notes so you can recognize them immediately.

Is your thumb curved properly on the bow?

MELODY IN 2/4 TIME

S. D. W.

2/4 Time - 2 beats to a measure, each quarter note gets one beat

Count   1 - 2   1 - 2

Keep the 1st finger down

MARCH

S. D. W.

Count 1   2   1   2

Tie means to play
both notes in one bow

USING THE SECOND FINGER

NOTE : In learning the first three notes of the scale, it is desirable to first sing the notes with Do, Re, Mi before playing them. This will help finger placement and intonation.

Sing first Do   Re   Mi

MELODY

L.H.   W. B.   U.H.   W.B.

L.H.   W. B.   U.H.   W.B.

Do   Re   Mi

Upbeat
Count   4   1   2   3   4

p means soft
f means loud

TONE STUDY

FINGER PLAY

Name the notes before playing them

S. D. W.

MARCH

S. D. W.

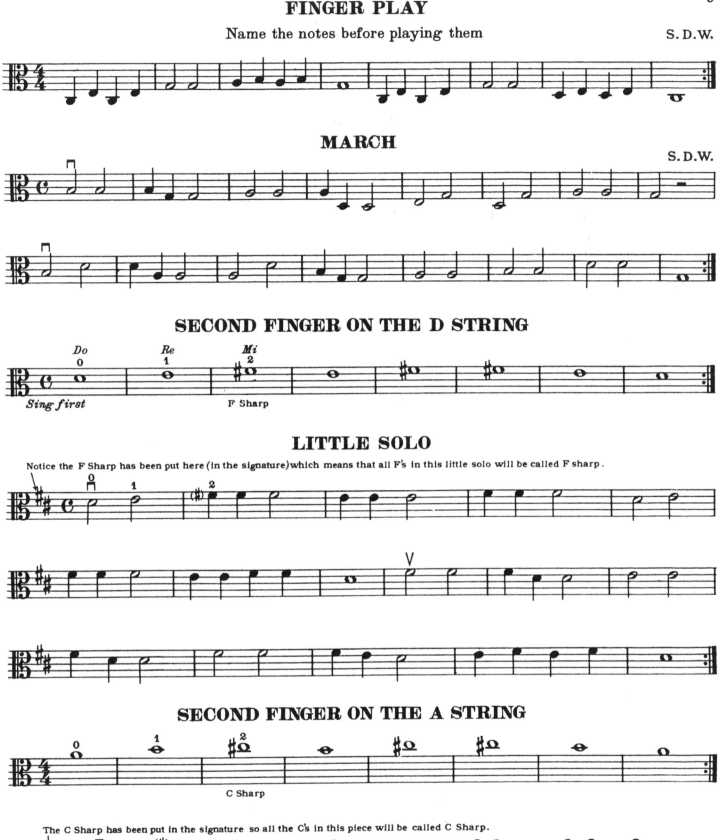

SECOND FINGER ON THE D STRING

Do 0   *Re* 1   *Mi* 2

Sing first   F Sharp

LITTLE SOLO

Notice the F Sharp has been put here (in the signature) which means that all F's in this little solo will be called F sharp.

SECOND FINGER ON THE A STRING

C Sharp

The C Sharp has been put in the signature so all the C's in this piece will be called C Sharp.

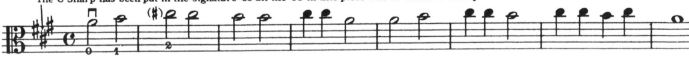

DOTTED HALF NOTES

A dot after a note increases the value of the note one half.

Count 1 2 3 4

ADDING THE THIRD FINGER

Half step between 2nd and 3rd finger

Repeat several times   Half step 3

0   1   2   G

Sing first   Do   Re   Mi   Fa

¾ TIME

¾ Time, 3 beats to a measure, each quarter note gets one beat.

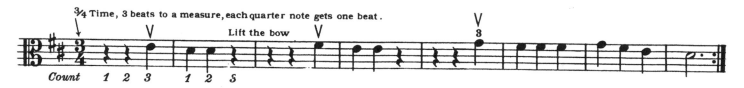

Count 1 2 3   1 2 3   Lift the bow

Keep the 3rd finger down

3   0

THIRD FINGER WALTZ

Gaily

S.D.W.

Count 1 2 3

Are you holding your right hand correctly?

Play short strokes just below middle of bow

THIRD FINGER ON THE G STRING

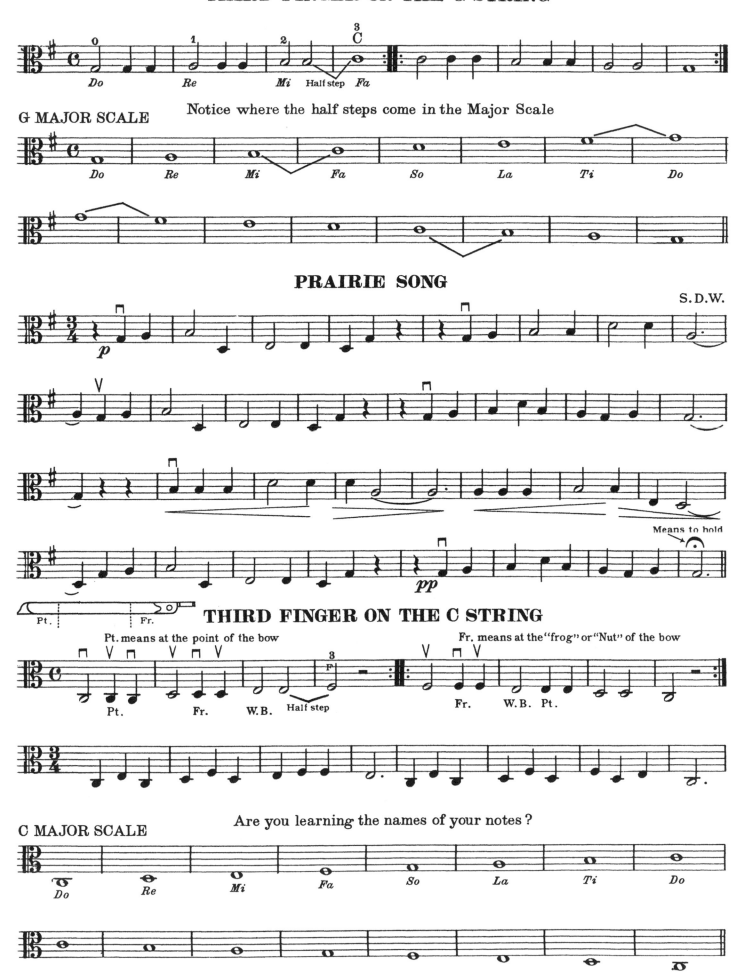

G MAJOR SCALE — Notice where the half steps come in the Major Scale

PRAIRIE SONG

S.D.W.

Means to hold

THIRD FINGER ON THE C STRING

Pt. means at the point of the bow — Fr. means at the "frog" or "Nut" of the bow

C MAJOR SCALE — Are you learning the names of your notes?

THE SLUR
Connects two or more notes in a bow

THIRD FINGER ON THE A STRING
Is your thumb curved properly on the bow?

D MAJOR SCALE

EIGHTH NOTES

ADDING THE FOURTH FINGER

Repeat on all strings

Practice both bowings – Play exercise on all strings.

FAMILIAR MELODY ON THE G STRING

Is your left wrist in the correct position?

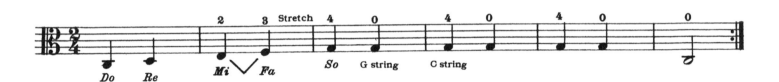

FOURTH FINGER MELODY

S.D.W.

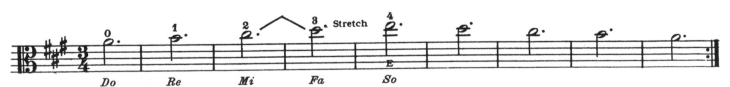

DOTTED QUARTER NOTES

Count 1 and 2 and 3 and 4 and

SOLO

GERMAN FOLK SONG

Play fingers as marked for practice

L.H.   W.B.   U.H.   W.B.   L.H.   U.H.   U.H.   L.H.

LEGATO

Stop the bow slightly
before playing the quarter note

M.

WALTZ

S. D. W.

LARGO

Slow — use long bows

DVORAK

EXERCISE IN HALF STEPS

Half step

Keep 1st finger down

This is called a "natural" and it cancels the sharp. Therefore you must move your second finger back near the first finger.

Stretch

Practice naming your notes before playing them

MELODY IN A MINOR KEY

Stretch

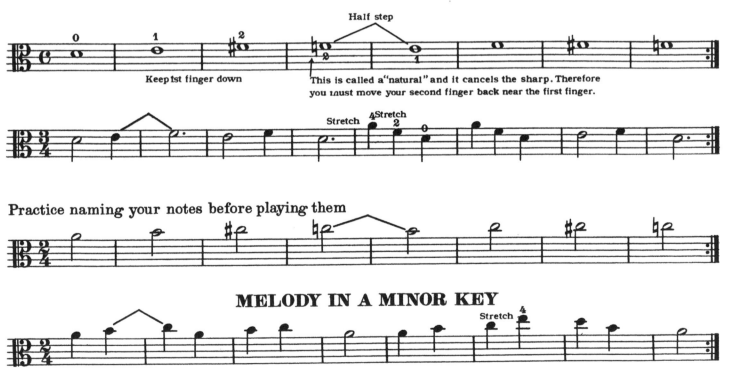

THIRDS

STACCATO

Keep the bow on the string - Move it quickly - Stop it quickly

OUR OLD CLOCK

S.D.W.

ALLA BREVE TIME

Quickens the time. Means each half note gets one beat.

Count 1 - 2

MARCH CADET

S. D. W.

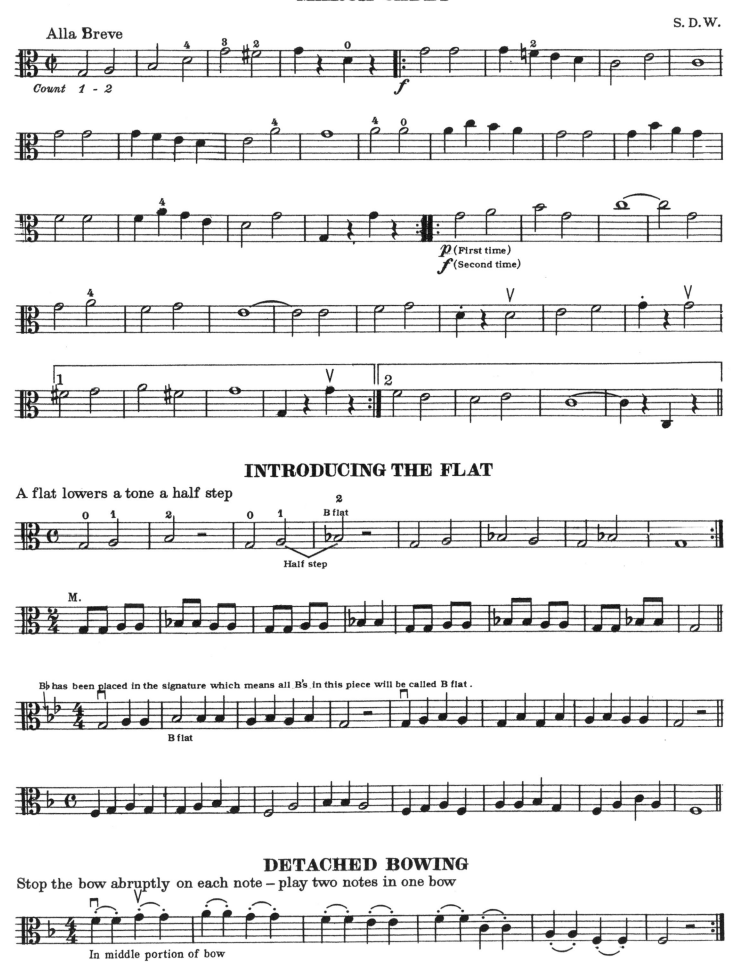

INTRODUCING THE FLAT

A flat lowers a tone a half step

DETACHED BOWING

Stop the bow abruptly on each note – play two notes in one bow

In middle portion of bow

F MAJOR SCALE

Do Re Mi Fa So La Ti Do

6/8 TIME

Clap rhythm with hands before playing, slightly accenting the first and fourth notes

Count 1 - 2 - 3 - 4-5-6
or   1 - 2

MARCH AWAY

S. D. W.

Count 1 - 2 - 3 - 4-5-6
or   1 - 2

CROSSING THE STRINGS

LULLABY

S. D. W.

PLAYING E FLAT ON THE C STRING

E♭ has been put in the signature, so all E's in this piece will be called E Flat.

WALTZ IN MINOR MODE

S. D. W.

AMERICA THE BEAUTIFUL

SAMUEL A. WARD

BOWING TWO STRINGS AT ONE TIME
(Double Stops)

SHE'LL BE COMIN' 'ROUND THE MOUNTAIN

BOWING EXERCISES

WRIST BOWING

VARIATIONS ON THE SCALE

A MAJOR SCALE

Practice all bowings

Come down scale
in same manner.

Also practice slurring the 1st two notes in the measure; last 2 notes; 1st 3 notes; last 3 notes; 4 notes in a bow.

Draw 1st
finger back

SINGING STRINGS

S.D.W.

FUN WITH INTERVALS

Always notice your key signature

START AND STOP

Stop the bow for each staccato note

ABIDE WITH ME

WILLIAM H. MONK

Draw 1st
finger back

FINGERING EXERCISES IN B FLAT MAJOR

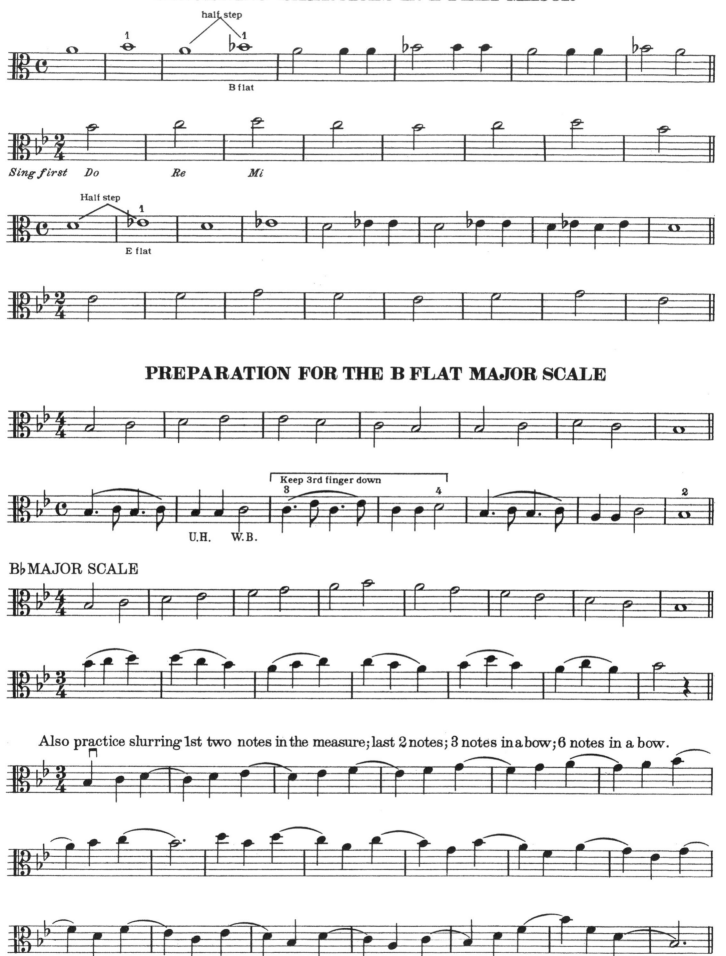

PREPARATION FOR THE B FLAT MAJOR SCALE

B♭ MAJOR SCALE

Also practice slurring 1st two notes in the measure; last 2 notes; 3 notes in a bow; 6 notes in a bow.

SIXTEENTH NOTES

GRASSHOPPER HOP

Practice slowly in the middle of the bow, then increase tempo.

S.D.W.

DOTTED SIXTEENTH NOTES

Repeat several times. (Try clapping the rhythm before playing)

OH! SUSANNA

STEPHEN C. FOSTER

Count and 1 and 2 and

DRINK TO ME ONLY WITH THINE EYES

OLD ENGLISH

STUDY IN HALF STEPS

This Natural cancels the flat so move your second finger up one half step

39118

PLAYING TRIPLETS

Try clapping the rhythm before playing

ACCENTS

Accents are procured by putting momentary pressure on the bow, causing a quick "bite" or "attack" of the string

Accent as marked

ETUDE

S.D.W.

Practice with and without the accents on the quarter notes.

PIZZICATO (Plucking the Strings)

Pluck the string with the forefinger of the right hand, allowing the bow to rest against the palm with the hair turned away from the string. Place the thumb down on the edge of the fingerboard near the A string. On short pizzicato passages, hold the bow as when bowing on the string and merely extend the forefinger, plucking the string with the fleshy part of the finger.

AMARYLLIS GAVOTTE

Allegro moderato

KING LOUIS XIII

JINGLE BELLS

J. PIERPONT

ETUDE

S.D.W.

Also play

DEEP RIVER

Lento

American Negro Spiritual

STRENGTHENING THE FOURTH FINGER

Count 1 - 2 - 3

Do you always look at your key signature before you play?

Do   Re   Mi   Fa   So

WHERE IS MY LITTLE DOG GONE?

Allegro

GERMAN SONG

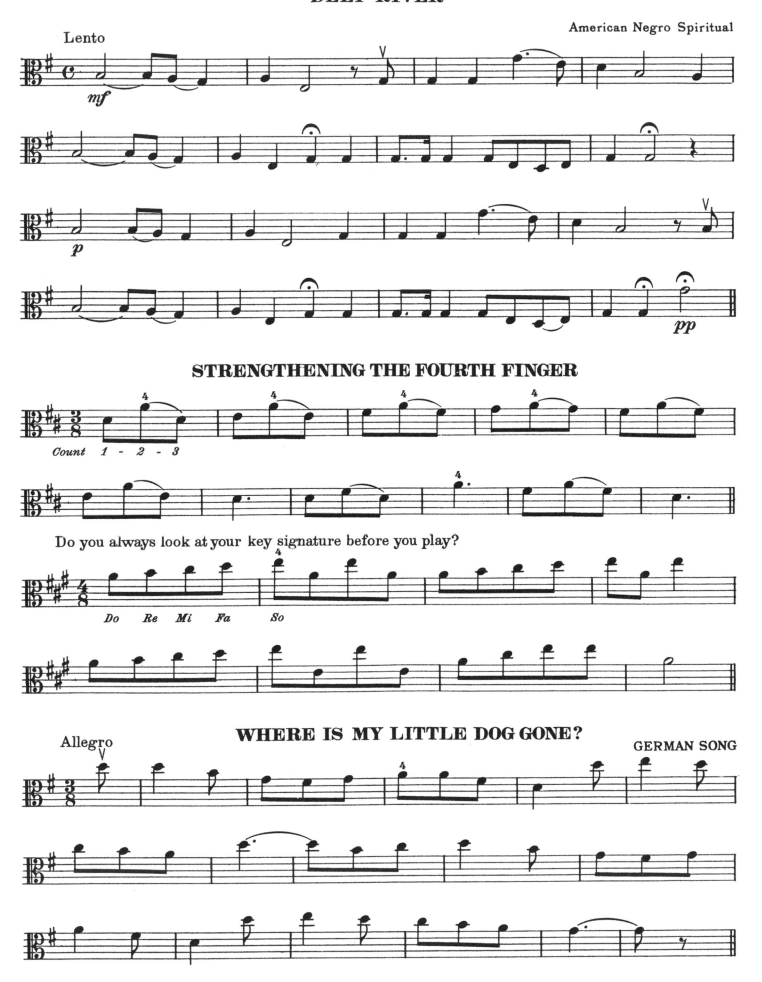

PLAYING IN E♭ MAJOR

Are you learning your sharps and flats as you go along so you know how many there are in each different scale you play?

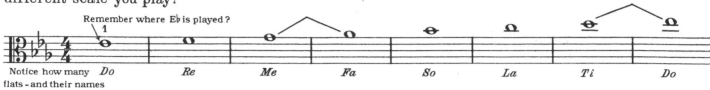

Remember where E♭ is played?

Notice how many flats - and their names: Do Re Me Fa So La Ti Do

Smoothly and evenly

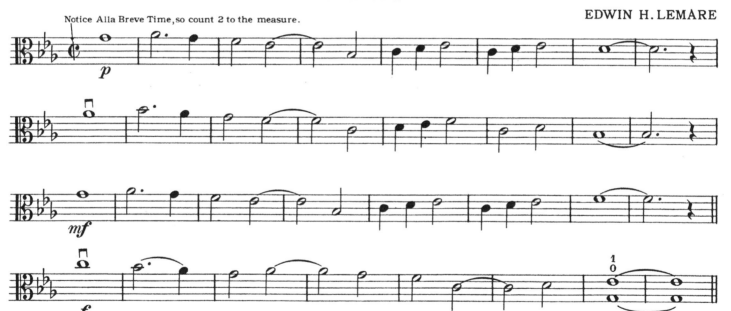

ANDANTINO

EDWIN H. LEMARE

Notice Alla Breve Time, so count 2 to the measure.

C MINOR

Notice where the half steps are in the Minor scale. Are they in the same places coming down the scale?

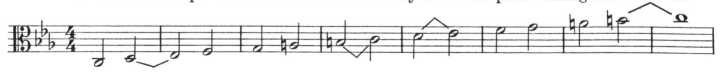

Compare the half steps in the Minor scale with those in the Major scale at the top of the page.

PLAYING IN E MAJOR

Notice how many sharps there are.

Do Re Mi Fa So La Ti Do Do Mi Do Mi

PUTTING RHYTHM IN THE SCALE

1. Are you holding your left hand correctly?
2. Is your right thumb curved properly on the bow?

SYNCOPATION

Count 1 and 2 and 3 and 4 and

SYNCOPATIN' SAM

S. D. W.

HALF STEP WALTZ

S. D. W.

PLAYING IN A FLAT MAJOR

Slowly at first

F Minor

MARCH SLAV

TSCHAIKOWSKY

Vigorously

DOTTED SIXTEENTH NOTE ETUDE

Stop the bow shortly on each note

S. D.W.

TIN SOLDIER PARADE

S. D.W.

LEARNING THE TRILL

Also practice using other fingers on different notes and strings.

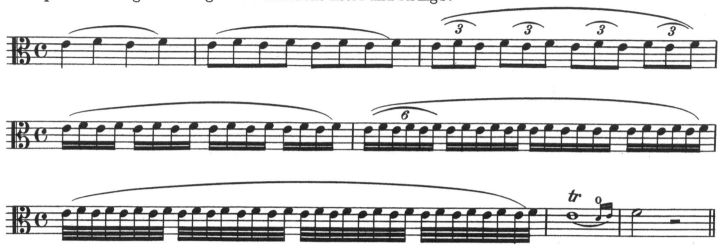

EXERCISE IN DOUBLE STOPS

Andante

For practice, first play the double stop without the sixteenth notes.

CHORDS

CHROMATIC WALTZ

THINK YOUR INTERVALS

Practice slowly, then increase tempo

CHROMATIC SCALE

WALTZ DORRELL

S. D. W.

NONE BUT THE LONELY HEART

PETER TSCHAIKOWSKY

MAJOR AND MINOR SCALES

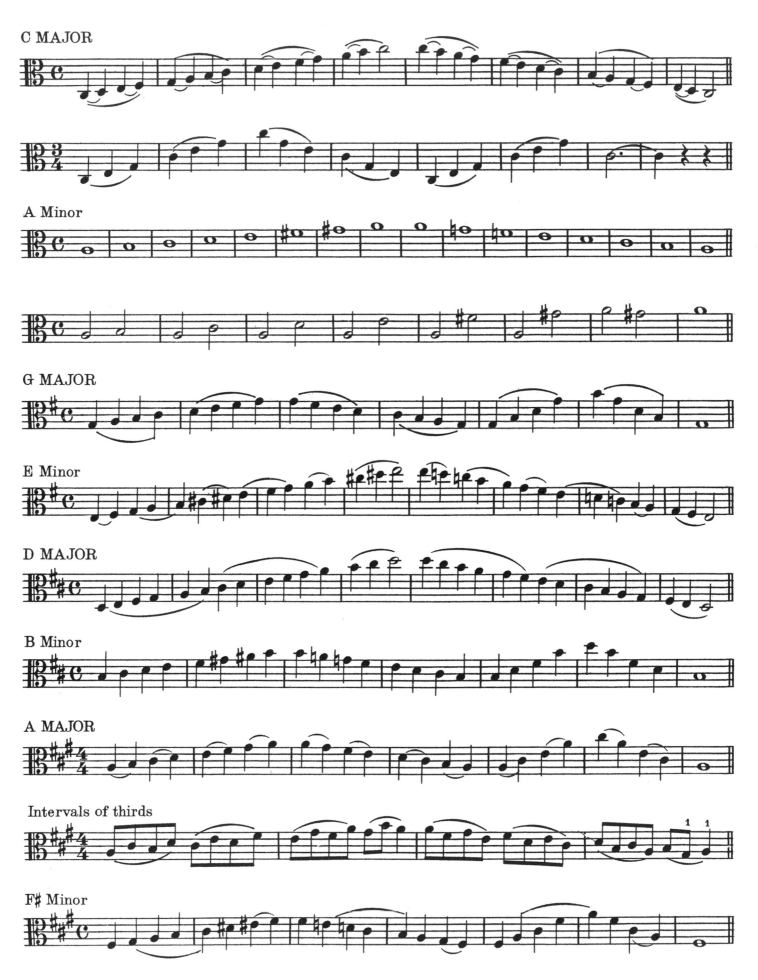

C MAJOR

A Minor

G MAJOR

E Minor

D MAJOR

B Minor

A MAJOR

Intervals of thirds

F♯ Minor

E MAJOR

Intervals of Fourths

C# Minor

B MAJOR

G# Minor

F MAJOR

Intervals of Fifths

D Minor

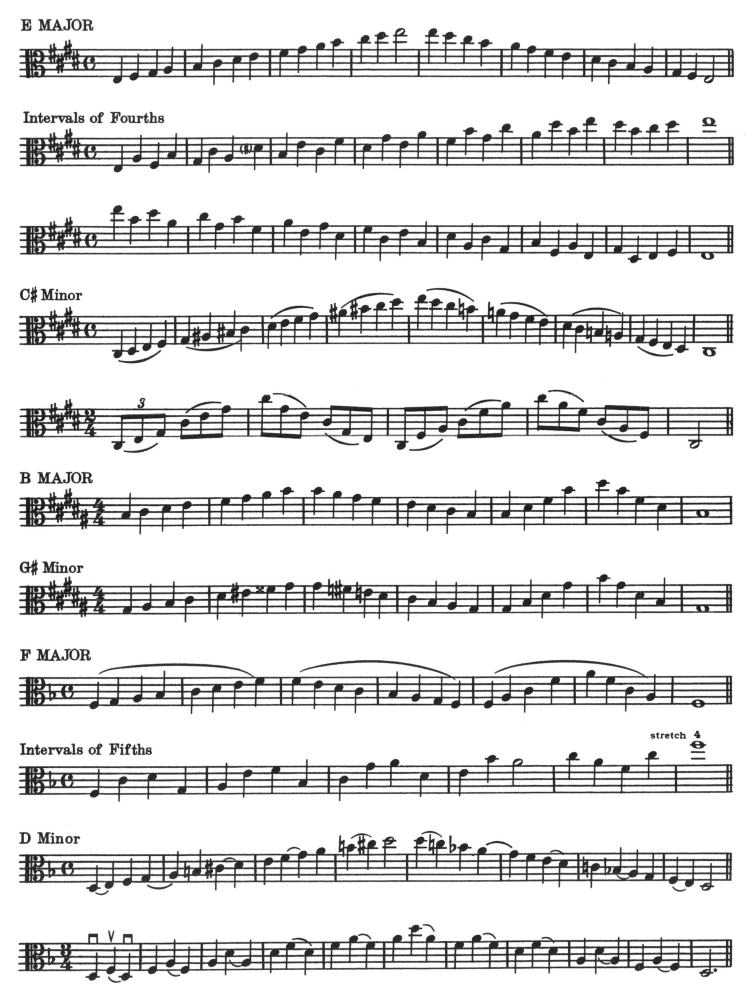

Bb MAJOR

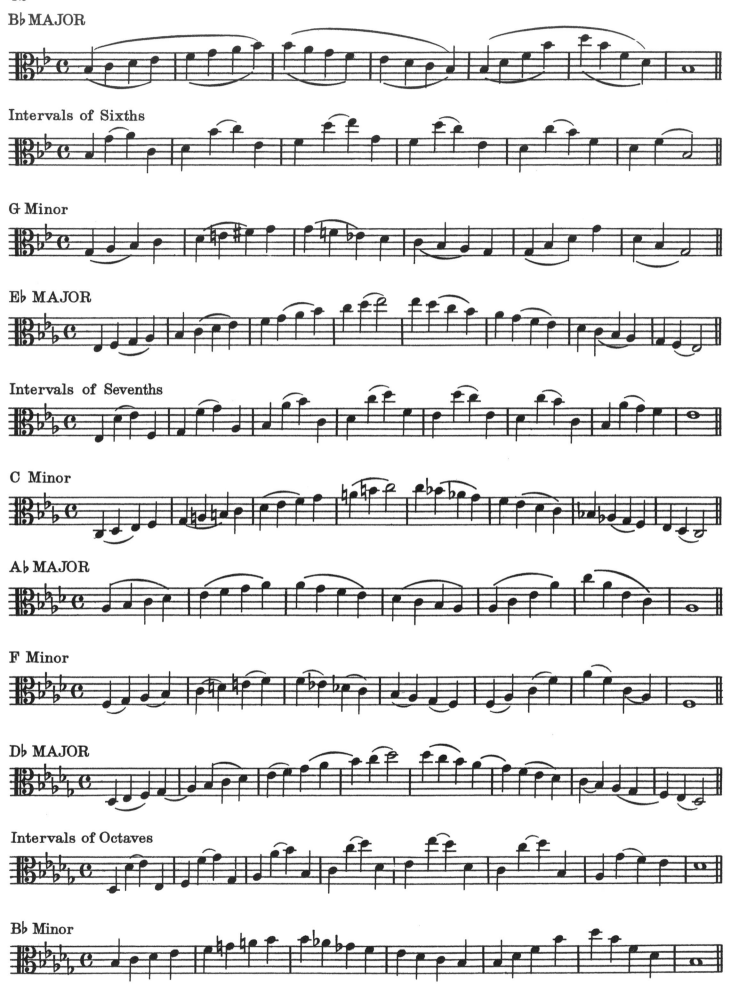

Intervals of Sixths

G Minor

Eb MAJOR

Intervals of Sevenths

C Minor

Ab MAJOR

F Minor

Db MAJOR

Intervals of Octaves

Bb Minor

BRAHM'S LULLABY

(Duet)

Arr. R.C.W.

ROW, ROW, ROW YOUR BOAT

(Round for 2, 3 or 4 Violas)

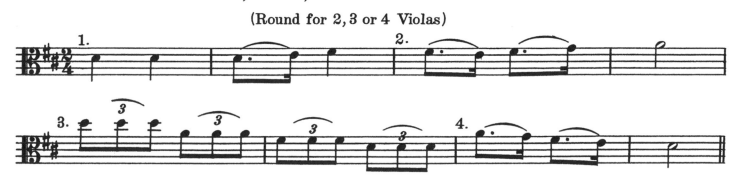

O SOLE MIO
(Duet)

E. DI CAPUA

SILENT NIGHT

FRANZ GRUBER

LITTLE MOUNTAIN MAID

(Fox Trot)

S.D.W.

PEASANT SONG

S.D.W.

THE QUAKING ASP

S. D. W.

I'LL TAKE YOU HOME AGAIN KATHLEEN

(Trio)

THOMAS P. WESTENDORF
Arr. by S. D. W.